BRITISH LIBRARY
DIARY
2018

F FRANCES LINCOLN

Front Cover: **Koala bears** by John William Lewin, from *Hindoostan Quadrupeds*, 1798–1805 [NHD 33/40]
Back Cover: **Tawny owl** by George Edwards, from *Drawing of Birds*, first half of the 18th century [Add. 5263, f.20]
Title page: **Black-billed darter** by John James Audubon, from *The Birds of America*, 1827–38 [N.L.TAB.2]
Left: **Palm squirrel**, from the Wellesley Albums, 1798–1805 [NHD 32/38]

Frances Lincoln Limited
74–77 White Lion Street
London N1 9PF

The British Library Diary 2018
Copyright © Frances Lincoln Limited 2017
Images and text © The British Library 2017

Astronomical information © Crown Copyright.
Reproduced by permission of the Controller of Her Majesty's Stationery Office and the UK Hydrographic Office (www.ukho.gov.uk)

A catalogue record for this book is available from the British Library

Designed by Arianna Osti

ISBN 978-0-7112-3878-7

Printed and bound in China

9 8 7 6 5 4 3 2 1

Quarto is the authority on a wide range of topics.

Quarto educates, entertains and enriches the lives of our readers – enthusiasts and lovers of hands-on living.

www.QuartoKnows.com

MIX
Paper from responsible sources
FSC® C008047

CALENDAR 2018

JANUARY
M	T	W	T	F	S	S
1	2	3	4	5	6	7
8	9	10	11	12	13	14
15	16	17	18	19	20	21
22	23	24	25	26	27	28
29	30	31				

FEBRUARY
M	T	W	T	F	S	S
			1	2	3	4
5	6	7	8	9	10	11
12	13	14	15	16	17	18
19	20	21	22	23	24	25
26	27	28				

MARCH
M	T	W	T	F	S	S
			1	2	3	4
5	6	7	8	9	10	11
12	13	14	15	16	17	18
19	20	21	22	23	24	25
26	27	28	29	30	31	

APRIL
M	T	W	T	F	S	S
						1
2	3	4	5	6	7	8
9	10	11	12	13	14	15
16	17	18	19	20	21	22
23	24	25	26	27	28	29
30						

MAY
M	T	W	T	F	S	S
	1	2	3	4	5	6
7	8	9	10	11	12	13
14	15	16	17	18	19	20
21	22	23	24	25	26	27
28	29	30	31			

JUNE
M	T	W	T	F	S	S
				1	2	3
4	5	6	7	8	9	10
11	12	13	14	15	16	17
18	19	20	21	22	23	24
25	26	27	28	29	30	

JULY
M	T	W	T	F	S	S
						1
2	3	4	5	6	7	8
9	10	11	12	13	14	15
16	17	18	19	20	21	22
23	24	25	26	27	28	29
30	31					

AUGUST
M	T	W	T	F	S	S
		1	2	3	4	5
6	7	8	9	10	11	12
13	14	15	16	17	18	19
20	21	22	23	24	25	26
27	28	29	30	31		

SEPTEMBER
M	T	W	T	F	S	S
					1	2
3	4	5	6	7	8	9
10	11	12	13	14	15	16
17	18	19	20	21	22	23
24	25	26	27	28	29	30

OCTOBER
M	T	W	T	F	S	S
1	2	3	4	5	6	7
8	9	10	11	12	13	14
15	16	17	18	19	20	21
22	23	24	25	26	27	28
29	30	31				

NOVEMBER
M	T	W	T	F	S	S
			1	2	3	4
5	6	7	8	9	10	11
12	13	14	15	16	17	18
19	20	21	22	23	24	25
26	27	28	29	30		

DECEMBER
M	T	W	T	F	S	S
					1	2
3	4	5	6	7	8	9
10	11	12	13	14	15	16
17	18	19	20	21	22	23
24	25	26	27	28	29	30
31						

CALENDAR 2019

JANUARY
M	T	W	T	F	S	S
	1	2	3	4	5	6
7	8	9	10	11	12	13
14	15	16	17	18	19	20
21	22	23	24	25	26	27
28	29	30	31			

FEBRUARY
M	T	W	T	F	S	S
				1	2	3
4	5	6	7	8	9	10
11	12	13	14	15	16	17
18	19	20	21	22	23	24
25	26	27	28			

MARCH
M	T	W	T	F	S	S
				1	2	3
4	5	6	7	8	9	10
11	12	13	14	15	16	17
18	19	20	21	22	23	24
25	26	27	28	29	30	31

APRIL
M	T	W	T	F	S	S
1	2	3	4	5	6	7
8	9	10	11	12	13	14
15	16	17	18	19	20	21
22	23	24	25	26	27	28
29	30					

MAY
M	T	W	T	F	S	S
		1	2	3	4	5
6	7	8	9	10	11	12
13	14	15	16	17	18	19
20	21	22	23	24	25	26
27	28	29	30	31		

JUNE
M	T	W	T	F	S	S
					1	2
3	4	5	6	7	8	9
10	11	12	13	14	15	16
17	18	19	20	21	22	23
24	25	26	27	28	29	30

JULY
M	T	W	T	F	S	S
1	2	3	4	5	6	7
8	9	10	11	12	13	14
15	16	17	18	19	20	21
22	23	24	25	26	27	28
29	30	31				

AUGUST
M	T	W	T	F	S	S
			1	2	3	4
5	6	7	8	9	10	11
12	13	14	15	16	17	18
19	20	21	22	23	24	25
26	27	28	29	30	31	

SEPTEMBER
M	T	W	T	F	S	S
						1
2	3	4	5	6	7	8
9	10	11	12	13	14	15
16	17	18	19	20	21	22
23	24	25	26	27	28	29
30						

OCTOBER
M	T	W	T	F	S	S
	1	2	3	4	5	6
7	8	9	10	11	12	13
14	15	16	17	18	19	20
21	22	23	24	25	26	27
28	29	30	31			

NOVEMBER
M	T	W	T	F	S	S
				1	2	3
4	5	6	7	8	9	10
11	12	13	14	15	16	17
18	19	20	21	22	23	24
25	26	27	28	29	30	

DECEMBER
M	T	W	T	F	S	S
						1
2	3	4	5	6	7	8
9	10	11	12	13	14	15
16	17	18	19	20	21	22
23	24	25	26	27	28	29
30	31					

INTRODUCTION

The *British Library Diary 2018* gathers together a selection of beautiful and fascinating images from the library's collection of natural history illustrations.

Art and illustration have for years played an important role in the development of science, particularly before the advent of photography. Recording and capturing fine detail is key to a successful and useful picture, but the images are far from clinical representations and can be enjoyed as works of art in their own right.

Numerous notable figures and key publications are included here: Swiss physician and naturalist Conrad Gessner (1516–65), whose encyclopedic *Historiæ animalium* is often regarded as the starting point of modern zoology; pioneering German artist Maria Sibilla Merian (1647–1717), one of the first naturalists to study insects; noted ornithologist George Edwards (1614–1773), whose publication *A Natural History of Uncommon Birds* did much to popularize the art of bird and animal illustration; painter and naturalist John James Audubon (1785–1851), creator of the seminal work *Birds of America* printed between 1827 and 1838; and English ornithologist John Gould (1804–81), whose work is referenced in Charles Darwin's *On the Origin of Species*.

These are beautifully realized and often striking images with great scientific, artistic and historic value. Sourced from manuscripts, journals and rare printed books, this collection offers a glimpse into some of the many zoological treasures to be found at the British Library.

Flamingo by Charles Reuben Ryley, from George Shaw's *Musei Leveriani explicatio, Anglica et Latina*, 1792 [40.e.15, plate opposite p.134]

JANUARY

01 *Monday*

New Year's Day
Holiday, UK, Republic of Ireland, USA, Canada,
Australia and New Zealand

02 *Tuesday*

Full moon
Holiday, Scotland and New Zealand

03 *Wednesday*

04 *Thursday*

05 *Friday*

06 *Saturday*

Epiphany

07 *Sunday*

Macaque by George Edwards, from *A Natural History of Uncommon Birds*, 1743–51
[435.g.3 p.197]

MAVCAVCO DICT:
197

JANUARY

Last quarter

Monday 08

Tuesday 09

Wednesday 10

Thursday 11

Friday 12

Saturday 13

Sunday 14

Parakeet by George Edwards, from *Drawings of Birds*, first half of the 18th century
[Add. 5263, f.61]

JANUARY

15 *Monday*   Holiday, USA (Martin Luther King Jnr Day)

16 *Tuesday*

17 *Wednesday*   *New moon*

18 *Thursday*

19 *Friday*

20 *Saturday*

21 *Sunday*

African land tortoise and small spotted grey lizard by George Shaw, from *A Natural History of Uncommon Birds*, 1743–51 [435.g.3 p.204]

JANUARY

22 *Monday*

23 *Tuesday*

24 *Wednesday*   *First quarter*

---

25 *Thursday*

---

26 *Friday*   Holiday, Australia (Australia Day)

---

27 *Saturday*

---

28 *Sunday*

Red-necked wallaby by John Gould, from *The Mammals of Australia*, 1845–63
[462*.e.4, vol.II, plate 17]

JANUARY / FEBRUARY

29 *Monday*

30 *Tuesday*

31 *Wednesday*   *Full moon*

01 *Thursday*

02 *Friday*

The Syrian goat by Elizabeth Sibley, from *An Universal System of Natural History*, 1794–1807
[1509/871, vol.III, plate opposite p.145]

03 *Saturday*

04 *Sunday*

FEBRUARY

Monday 05

Accession of Queen Elizabeth II
Holiday, New Zealand (Waitangi Day)

Tuesday 06

Last quarter

Wednesday 07

Thursday 08

Friday 09

Saturday 10

Sunday 11

Snowy owl by John James Audubon, from *The Birds of America*, 1827–38
[N.L.TAB.2.(2) plate 121]

FEBRUARY

12 *Monday*

13 *Tuesday*   Shrove Tuesday

14 *Wednesday*   Valentine's Day
Ash Wednesday

15 *Thursday*   *New moon*

16 *Friday*   Chinese New Year

17 *Saturday*

18 *Sunday*

Guana or *Anona maxima* by Mark Catesby, from *The Natural History of Carolina, Florida and the Bahama Islands*, 1731–43 [44.k.8, plate 64]

FEBRUARY

Holiday, USA (Presidents' Day)

Monday 19

Tuesday 20

Wednesday 21

Thursday 22

First quarter

Friday 23

Saturday 24

Sunday 25

Koala bears by John Gould, from *The Mammals of Australia*, 1845–63
[462*.e.4, vol.1, plate 14]

FEBRUARY / MARCH

26 *Monday*

27 *Tuesday*

28 *Wednesday*

01 *Thursday*   St David's Day

02 *Friday*   *Full moon*

03 *Saturday*

04 *Sunday*

Long-headed African locust by Frederick Polydore Nodder, from *The Naturalists' Miscellany*, 1789–1813 [45.b.3 plate 784]

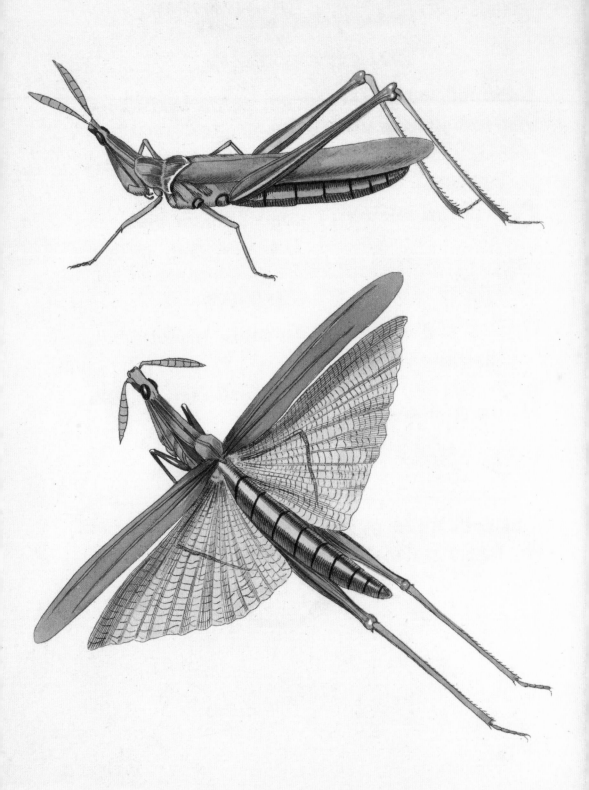

MARCH

Monday 05

Tuesday 06

Wednesday 07

Thursday 08

Last quarter

Friday 09

Saturday 10

Mother's Day, UK and Republic of Ireland

Sunday 11

Bird of Paradise by Jacques Barraband, from *Histoire Naturelle des Oiseaux de Paradis et des Rolliers*, 1806 [39.i.7-8 plate 16]

MARCH

12 *Monday*   Commonwealth Day

13 *Tuesday*

14 *Wednesday*

15 *Thursday*

16 *Friday*

Domestic goat, from the Wellesley Albums, 1798–1805 [NHD 32/89]

17 *Saturday*

18 *Sunday*

Holiday, Northern Ireland and Republic of Ireland
(St Patrick's Day)

Monday 19

Vernal Equinox (Spring begins)

Tuesday 20

Wednesday 21

Thursday 22

Friday 23

First quarter

Saturday 24

Palm Sunday
British Summer Time begins

Sunday 25

Meadowlarks by John James Audubon, from *The Birds of America*, 1827–38
[N.L.TAB.2.(2) plate 136]

MARCH / APRIL

---

26 *Monday*

---

27 *Tuesday*

---

28 *Wednesday*

---

29 *Thursday*   Maundy Thursday

---

30 *Friday*   Good Friday
Holiday, UK, Canada, Australia and New Zealand

---

31 *Saturday*   *Full moon*
Holiday, Australia (Easter Saturday)
First day of Passover (Pesach)

---

01 *Sunday*   Easter Sunday

Birds' eggs by Johann Friedrich Naumann, from *The Birds of Central Europe
and their Eggs*, 1880–1 [7284.i.3 plate X]

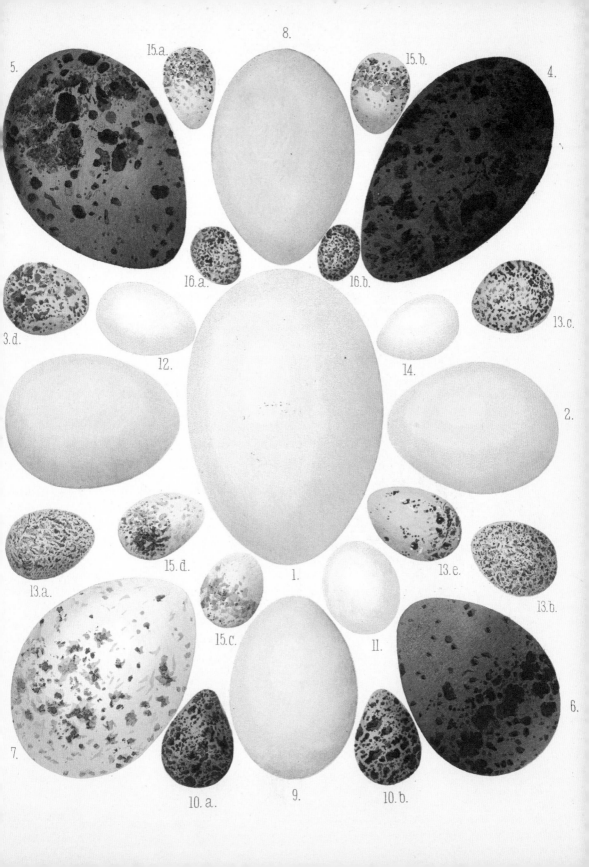

Merops viridis

183

Easter Monday
Holiday, UK (exc. Scotland), Republic of Ireland,
Australia and New Zealand

Monday 02

Tuesday 03

Wednesday 04

Thursday 05

Friday 06

Saturday 07

Last quarter

Sunday 08

The Indian bee-eater by George Edwards, from *A Natural History of Uncommon Birds*, 1743–51
[435.g.3 p.183]

APRIL

09 *Monday*

10 *Tuesday*

11 *Wednesday*

12 *Thursday*

13 *Friday*

Tasmanian wolf by John Gould, from *The Mammals of Australia*, 1845–63
[462*.e.4, vol.I, plate 54]

14 *Saturday*

15 *Sunday*

APRIL

New moon

Monday 16

Tuesday 17

Wednesday 18

Thursday 19

Friday 20

Birthday of Queen Elizabeth II

Saturday 21

First quarter

Sunday 22

The bee-eater by Eleazar Albin, from *A Natural History of Birds*, 1738 [37.e.4 vol.II plate 44]

APRIL

23 *Monday* — St George's Day

24 *Tuesday*

25 *Wednesday* — Holiday, Australia and New Zealand (Anzac Day)

26 *Thursday*

27 *Friday*

28 *Saturday*

29 *Sunday*

European tree frog by Frederick Polydore Nodder, from *The Naturalists' Miscellany*, 1789–1813 [44.b.20 plate 127]

Full moon

Monday 30

Tuesday 01

Wednesday 02

Thursday 03

Friday 04

Saturday 05

Sunday 06

White bill'd woodpecker by Mark Catesby, from *The Natural History of Carolina, Florida and the Bahama Islands*, 1731–43 [44.k.7 plate T.16]

MAY

07 *Monday*

Early Spring Bank Holiday, UK
Holiday, Republic of Ireland

08 *Tuesday*

Last quarter

09 *Wednesday*

10 *Thursday*

Ascension Day

11 *Friday*

12 *Saturday*

13 *Sunday*

Mother's Day, USA, Canada,
Australia and New Zealand

Winged insects by Du Drury, from *Illustrations of Natural History*, 1770–82 [38.e.12 plate XLVI]

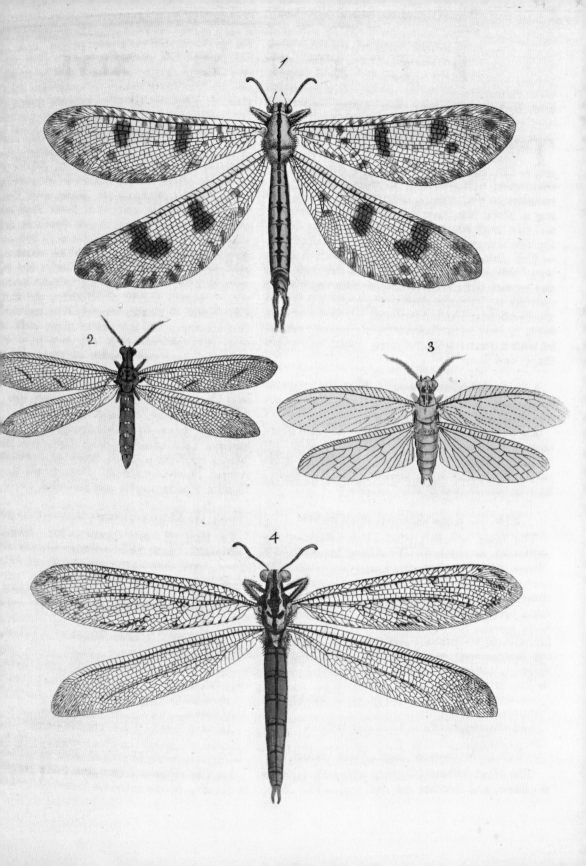

MAY

Monday 14

New moon

Tuesday 15

First day of Ramadân
(subject to sighting of the moon)

Wednesday 16

Thursday 17

Friday 18

Saturday 19

Whit Sunday
Feast of Weeks (Shavuot)

Sunday 20

Cockatoo by George Edwards, from *Drawings of Birds*, first half of the 18th century
[Add. 5263, f.49]

MAY

21 *Monday*   Holiday, Canada (Victoria Day)

22 *Tuesday*   *First quarter*

23 *Wednesday*

24 *Thursday*

25 *Friday*

Field mice by William MacGillivray, from *A History of British Quadrupeds*, 1843
[1150.a.7 plate opposite p.254]

26 *Saturday*

27 *Sunday*

Trinity Sunday

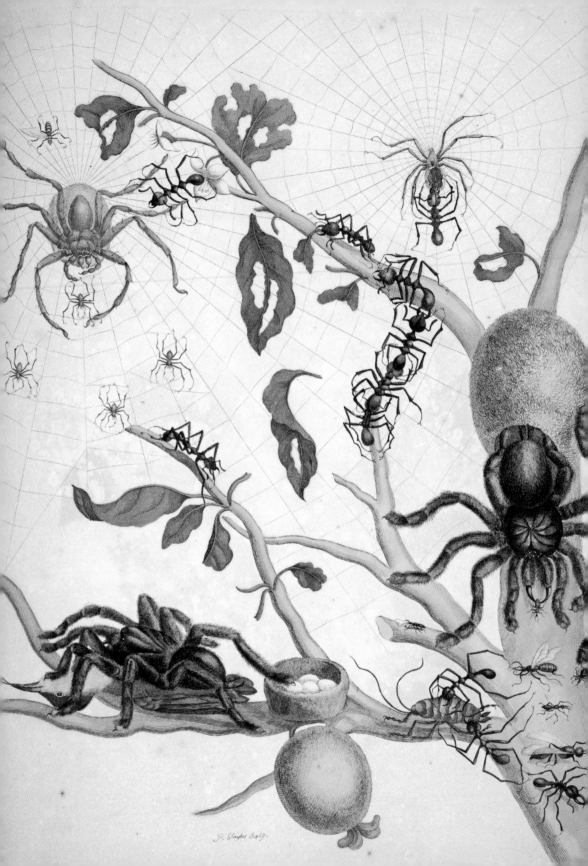

MAY / JUNE

Spring Bank Holiday, UK
Holiday, USA (Memorial Day)

Monday 28

Full moon

Tuesday 29

Wednesday 30

Corpus Christi

Thursday 31

Friday 01

Coronation Day

Saturday 02

Sunday 03

Spiders and ants by Maria Sibilla Merian, from *Metamorphosis insectorum*, 1705
[649.c.26 plate 18]

JUNE

04 *Monday*

Holiday, Republic of Ireland
Holiday, New Zealand (The Queen's Birthday)

05 *Tuesday*

06 *Wednesday*

Last quarter

07 *Thursday*

08 *Friday*

09 *Saturday*

The Queen's Official Birthday
(subject to confirmation)

10 *Sunday*

Peacock pheasant from China by George Edwards, from *A Natural History of Uncommon Birds*, 1743–51 [435.g.4.(ii), plate 67]

Published Decemr 1745

67

G Edwards

Pavo~bicalcaratus.

Camellia Japonica Lin

JUNE

Holiday, Australia (The Queen's Birthday)

Monday 11

Tuesday 12

New moon

Wednesday 13

Thursday 14

Eid al-Fitr (end of Ramadân)
(subject to sighting of the moon)

Friday 15

Saturday 16

Father's Day, UK, Republic of Ireland,
USA and Canada

Sunday 17

Butterfly and caterpillar by Maria Sibilla Merian, from *Metamorphosis insectorum*, 1705
[649.c.26, plate 12]

JUNE

18 *Monday*

19 *Tuesday*

20 *Wednesday*   *First quarter*

21 *Thursday*   Summer Solstice (Summer begins)

22 *Friday*

23 *Saturday*

24 *Sunday*

American White Pelican by John James Audubon, from *The Birds of America*, 1827–38
[N.L.TAB.2.(3) plate 311]

JUNE / JULY

Monday 25

Tuesday 26

Wednesday 27

Full moon

Thursday 28

Friday 29

Saturday 30

Canada Day

Sunday 01

Reindeer by Conrad Gessner, from *Historiæ animalium*, 1551–87 [460.c.1 p.1100]

JULY

02 *Monday*   Holiday, Canada (Canada Day)

---

03 *Tuesday*

---

04 *Wednesday*   Holiday, USA (Independence Day)

---

05 *Thursday*

---

06 *Friday*   *Last quarter*

Land crab and *tapia trifolio fructu* plant by Mark Catesby, from *The Natural History of Carolina, Florida and the Bahama Islands*, 1731–43 [44.k.8, plate 32]

07 *Saturday*

08 *Sunday*

The Bill Bird

Pica brasiliensis Toucan

64

Ramphastos-piscivorus

JULY

Monday 09

Tuesday 10

Wednesday 11

Holiday, Northern Ireland (Battle of the Boyne)　　　Thursday 12

New moon　　　Friday 13

Saturday 14

St Swithin's Day　　　Sunday 15

Toucan or Brazilian pye by George Edwards, from *A Natural History of Uncommon Birds*, 1743–51
[435.g.3 p.64]

JULY

16 *Monday*

17 *Tuesday*

18 *Wednesday*

19 *Thursday*   *First quarter*

20 *Friday*

Zebra by Elizabeth Sibley, from *An Universal System of Natural History*, 1794–1807
[1509/871, vol.III, plate opposite p.68]

21 *Saturday*

22 *Sunday*

JULY

Monday 23

Tuesday 24

Wednesday 25

Thursday 26

Full moon

Friday 27

Saturday 28

Sunday 29

Arctic tern by John James Audubon, from *The Birds of America*, 1827–38
[N.L.TAB.2.(3) plate 250]

JULY / AUGUST

30 *Monday*

31 *Tuesday*

01 *Wednesday*

02 *Thursday*

03 *Friday*

04 *Saturday*   *Last quarter*

05 *Sunday*

Toucan by Jacques Barraband, from *Histoire naturelle des Oiseaux de Paradis et des Rolliers*, 1806 [39.i.7-8 plate 2]

1

3.

1/2.

2/3

4.

C⁰ Nat

8.

2/3

AUGUST

Holiday, Scotland and Republic of Ireland

Monday 06

Tuesday 07

Wednesday 08

Thursday 09

Friday 10

New moon

Saturday 11

Sunday 12

Cichlid, surgeonfish, *clinus fasciatus* & *malthea notate* from *Animaux nouveaux ou rares recueillis pendant l'Expédition dans les parties centrales de l'Amérique du Sud*, by Francis L. de Laporte and Count de Casteinau, 1850 [1295.i.1 vol.II plate 12]

AUGUST

13 *Monday*

14 *Tuesday*

15 *Wednesday*

16 *Thursday*

17 *Friday*

Divers and coastal wanderers by John James Audubon, from *The Birds of America*, 1827–38
[N.L.TAB.2.(2) plate 210]

18 *Saturday*

First quarter

19 *Sunday*

AUGUST

Monday 20

Tuesday 21

Wednesday 22

Thursday 23

Friday 24

Saturday 25

Full moon

Sunday 26

Male American flamingo by John James Audubon, from *The Birds of America*, 1827–38
[N.L.TAB.2.(4) plate 431]

AUGUST / SEPTEMBER

27 *Monday*   Summer Bank Holiday, UK (exc. Scotland)

---

28 *Tuesday*

---

29 *Wednesday*

---

30 *Thursday*

---

31 *Friday*

The chain snake by Mark Catesby, from *The Natural History of Carolina, Florida and the Bahama Islands*, 1731–43 [44.k.8 vol.2, plate 52]

01 *Saturday*

02 *Sunday*   Father's Day, Australia and New Zealand

SEPTEMBER

Last quarter
Holiday, USA (Labor Day)
Holiday, Canada (Labour Day)

Monday 03

Tuesday 04

Wednesday 05

Thursday 06

Friday 07

Saturday 08

New moon

Sunday 09

Woodpeckers and pigeon by Alexander Lawson, from *American Ornithology*, 1825–33
[457.e.6-9, opposite p.75]

SEPTEMBER

10 *Monday*   Jewish New Year (Rosh Hashanah)

11 *Tuesday*

12 *Wednesday*   Islamic New Year

13 *Thursday*

14 *Friday*

15 *Saturday*

16 *Sunday*   *First quarter*

Various spiders and web by Eleazar Albin, from *Aranei; or a Natural History of Spiders*, 1793
[37.f.12, frontispiece]

Geo Edwards

198

SEPTEMBER

Monday 17

Tuesday 18

Day of Atonement (Yom Kippur)   *Wednesday* 19

Thursday 20

Friday 21

Saturday 22

Autumnal Equinox (Autumn begins)   *Sunday* 23

SEPTEMBER

24 *Monday*   First day of Tabernacles (Succoth)

25 *Tuesday*   *Full moon*

26 *Wednesday*

27 *Thursday*

28 *Friday*

29 *Saturday*   Michaelmas Day

30 *Sunday*

Peregrine falcon by Johann Andreas Naumann, from *Naturgeschichte der Vogel Mittel-Europas*, 1905 [7208.I.1 vol.III Band V plate 16]

J Mulder Sculp

OCTOBER

Monday 01

Last quarter

Tuesday 02

Wednesday 03

Thursday 04

Friday 05

Saturday 06

Sunday 07

Grapevine with feeding insects by Maria Sibilla Merian, from *Metamorphosis insectorum*, 1705 [649.c.26 p.47]

OCTOBER

08 *Monday*

Holiday, USA (Columbus Day)
Holiday, Canada (Thanksgiving)

09 *Tuesday*   *New moon*

10 *Wednesday*

11 *Thursday*

12 *Friday*

The umbrella tree by Mark Catesby, from *The Natural History of Carolina, Florida and the Bahama Islands*, 1731–43 [44.k.8 vol.2, plate 80]

13 *Saturday*

14 *Sunday*

OCTOBER

Monday 15

First quarter

Tuesday 16

Wednesday 17

Thursday 18

Friday 19

Saturday 20

Sunday 21

Moths and butterflies from *Episodes of Insect Life*, 1849–51 [C.109.c.4 vol.1 frontispiece]

OCTOBER

22 *Monday* Holiday, New Zealand (Labour Day)

23 *Tuesday*

24 *Wednesday* *Full moon*

25 *Thursday*

26 *Friday*

Smaller one-horned Javan rhinoceros, from the Wellesley Albums, 1798–1805 [NHD 32/46]

27 *Saturday*

28 *Sunday*   British Summer Time ends

one foot.

OCTOBER / NOVEMBER

Holiday, Republic of Ireland

Monday 29

Tuesday 30

Last quarter
Halloween

Wednesday 31

All Saints' Day

Thursday 01

Friday 02

Saturday 03

Sunday 04

Winged lizard by George Edwards, from *Amphibians and Reptiles*, first half of the 18th century [Add. 5272, f.27]

NOVEMBER

05 *Monday* Guy Fawkes

06 *Tuesday*

07 *Wednesday* New moon

08 *Thursday*

09 *Friday*

Spotted hyena from *An Universal System of Natural History* by Carl von Linné, 1794–1807
[1509/871, vol.III, plate opposite p.309]

10 *Saturday*

11 *Sunday*   Remembrance Sunday

NOVEMBER

Holiday, USA (Veterans Day)
Holiday, Canada (Remembrance Day)

Monday 12

Tuesday 13

Wednesday 14

First quarter

Thursday 15

Friday 16

Saturday 17

Sunday 18

Cocoon, pupa, caterpillar and butterfly by Maria Sibilla Merian, from *Metamorphosis insectorum*, 1705 [649.c.26 p. end 2]

NOVEMBER

19 *Monday*

20 *Tuesday*

21 *Wednesday*

22 *Thursday*   Holiday, USA (Thanksgiving)

23 *Friday*   *Full moon*

24 *Saturday*

25 *Sunday*

Woolly spider monkey by Waterhouse Hawkins, from *The Zoology of the Voyage of H.M.S. Sulphur*, 1843–45 [1255.k.5 plate 1]

Atlantic Right Whale.

Humpbacked Whale.

$\frac{1}{75}$

NOVEMBER / DECEMBER

Monday 26

Tuesday 27

Wednesday 28

Thursday 29

Last quarter
St Andrew's Day

Friday 30

Saturday 01

First Sunday in Advent
Hannukah begins (at sunset)

Sunday 02

Atlantic right whale and humbacked whale by Archibald Thorburn, from *British Mammals*, 1920–1 [LR.32.b.8, vol.II plate 42]

DECEMBER

03 *Monday*

04 *Tuesday*

05 *Wednesday*

06 *Thursday*

07 *Friday*   *New moon*

Male and female large billed puffins by John James Audubon, from *The Birds of America*, 1827–38 [N.L.TAB.2.(3) plate 293]

08 *Saturday*

09 *Sunday*

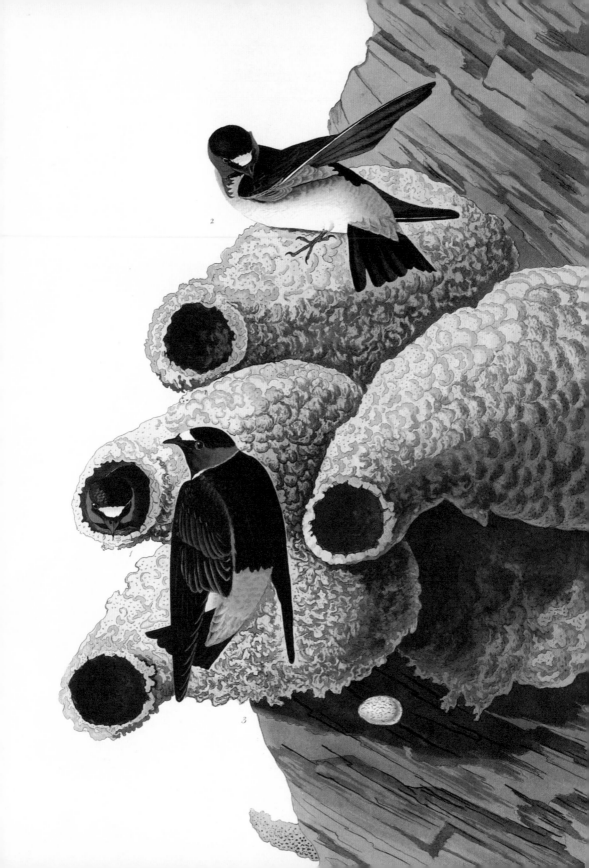

DECEMBER

Hannukah ends

Monday 10

Tuesday 11

Wednesday 12

Thursday 13

Friday 14

First quarter

Saturday 15

Sunday 16

Republican cliff swallows by John James Audubon, from *The Birds of America*, 1827–38
[N.L.TAB.2.(4) plate 68]

DECEMBER

17 *Monday*

18 *Tuesday*

19 *Wednesday*

20 *Thursday*

21 *Friday*   Winter Solstice (Winter begins)

22 *Saturday*   *Full moon*

23 *Sunday*

Long-armed gibbon by Charles Reuben Ryley, from George Shaw's *Musei Leveriani explicatio, Anglica et Latina*, 1792 [40.e.15 plate opposite p.55]

DECEMBER

Christmas Eve

Monday **24**

Christmas Day
Holiday, UK, Republic of Ireland, USA, Canada,
Australia and New Zealand

Tuesday **25**

Boxing Day (St Stephen's Day)
Holiday, UK, Republic of Ireland, Canada,
Australia and New Zealand

Wednesday **26**

Thursday **27**

Friday **28**

Last quarter

Saturday **29**

Sunday **30**

Columbia Jays by John James Audubon, from *The Birds of America*, 1827–38
[N.L.TAB.2.(1) plate 96]

DECEMBER / JANUARY

31 *Monday*   New Year's Eve

01 *Tuesday*   New Year's Day
Holiday, UK, Republic of Ireland, USA,
Canada, Australia and New Zealand

02 *Wednesday*   Holiday, Scotland and New Zealand

03 *Thursday*

04 *Friday*

05 *Saturday*

06 *Sunday*   *New moon*
Epiphany

Mountain hare in winter by Archibald Thorburn, from *British Mammals*, 1920–1
[LR.32.b.8, vol.II plate 35]

Mountain Hare. (winter)

NOTES